Life STORIES

Hope beyond Dementia

LESSONS FROM A PERSONAL JOURNEY OF CARE

DayOne

© Day One Publications 2024

ISBN 978-1-84625-780-3

British Library Cataloguing in Publication Data available

Scripture quotations in this publication are from the Holy Bible, New International Version (NIV), copyright © 1973, 1978, 1984, 2011, International Bible Society. Used by permission of Hodder and Stoughton, a member of the Hodder Headline Group. All rights reserved.

Published by Day One Publications
Ryelands Road, Leominster, HR6 8NZ
Telephone 01568 613 740
North America Toll Free 888 329 6630
email—sales@dayone.co.uk
web site—www.dayone.co.uk

All rights reserved
No part of this publication may be reproduced, or stored in a retrieval system, or transmitted, in any form or by any means, mechanical, electronic, photocopying, recording or otherwise, without the prior permission of Day One Publications.

Printed by 4edge Limited

Dedication

For my Dad

And to the God who saves

Contents

Introduction		6
1	Disease development	9
2	External help	27
3	Practical steps	31
4	Dealing with yourself	36
5	Dealing with the person	41
6	Spiritual aspect	46
7	End days	60
8	Afterwards	65
Acknowledgements and reference material		70

Introduction

In the summer of 2015, our world was turned upside down by the diagnosis that Dad had dementia—particularly, the form known as Alzheimer's. I, like many people, didn't understand the implications of what that entailed, nor had any idea of the process, journey, heartache, tears, anger, frustration, confusion and loneliness following that pronouncement. Life carried on as it had done. Weekends were busy, Dad appeared the same, plans and holidays were made, and all seemed superficially normal.

The only immediate change was that the doctor who made the assessment asked Dad what his driving was like. ('Exemplary. I've been driving for almost sixty years, full no-claims, etc., etc.') The doctor, turning to Dad's partner with the same question, received the response of, 'Well ... there was that time recently you went the wrong way round a roundabout ...'. Hearing this, the doctor recommended Dad restricted his driving to local, day-time only journeys. Dad flashed back at this, and so the doctor went a step further and told Dad he was no longer fit to drive, increasing Dad's anger at this loss of liberty.

After a number of days of not speaking to his partner we were able to discover that he'd have to sit a driving assessment at a specialist centre. In the meantime, he fumed at home, alone, reliant on the lifts of others, while his car was farmed out to the family. I later discovered that a limited driving scope as the doctor has recommended has no legal basis in the UK (unlike Australia)—it's a full licence or nothing.

Introduction

I undertook (in a complete role reversal) to coach Dad on how to drive, at a local airfield. As he demonstrated control of the car, I arranged to go with him to the test centre. In a worrying portent of things to come, he failed the theory and then the practical test. This plunged him into more anger management classes. It was a huge loss and completely knocked the wind out of his sails, impacting his confidence, life outlook, independence and relationships with others.

Looking back, we had no idea of what we were about to face. Feeling very alone and isolated, there was no immediate awareness of what to do, nor indeed was there a requirement for any initial action. There was, however, a sense of masses of information and support 'out there' and yet at the same time no idea where to start. Added to this was a sense of aloneness and feeling very helpless. Nobody was able to place a single source of clear, practical, concise guidance in our hand. Websites appeared overwhelming with their level of advice; all that was wanted was a person to take us by the hand and say, 'I've been there. Prepare yourself. Take things slowly. But put some plans into place...'. No simple, straightforward advice could be found. I later found some Christian literature on coping with dementia in a Christian relative, but nothing about a non-Christian relative; and nothing outlining some of the simple practical steps to take.

This book hopes to be a remedy for that. I hope it will help steer, guide, comfort and direct those in the early, middle or even latter stages of caring for a relative, friend, neighbour or colleague with dementia. There is hope. In your situation God is already there.

Previously as a family we had been through this with Mum in her battle with cancer (in a hospice). Then, as now, we made it up as we went along, picking up advice as we went, making decisions on the hoof. Some of what is outlined here I learned too late to implement; much was learnt as I went along, and many mistakes were made.

Introduction

I wish I'd been armed with this knowledge at the start as it would have would have helped a lot.

So, in summary, this book is aiming to do two things:
1. Offer practical help to those functioning as central carers.
2. Give encouragement on witnessing to a non-Christian person living with dementia.

To God be the glory.

Chris Gee
August 2024

Chapter 1

Disease development

In the time leading up to Dad's diagnosis he was increasingly becoming forgetful and unable to do some simple tasks, while his house slowly became more of a mess. His driving deteriorated too. However, as we were only involved on the periphery of his life it was difficult to quantify and see the full extent of what was happening; even Dad's partner was concerned but not able to fully appreciate or articulate the breadth of the issues Dad was starting to suffer with. He denied matters, put them down to being forgetful, always being like that, etc., etc. Life went on. Yet eventually the underlying murmurs of anxiety became louder and more frequent; matters became more pressing and so doctor's appointments were made which folks attended with him to help ensure all the facts were raised.

Following the diagnosis, we continued on with life as normal. I continued to run his car and use it to ferry him about, in the vain hope that things would get better and, somehow, he'd get back to driving. Inevitably, that didn't happen and the car was eventually sold back to the main dealer who had supplied it.

With no deliberate intention we kept life as routine as possible, only referring to the condition as 'early-stage' dementia, thinking that its development was many years in the future. Dad refused to acknowledge his condition. This living in denial rubbed off on us too, in part. We didn't want to force the issue, nor be cruel in making him admit to it. In hindsight, early acknowledgement would have helped confirm the diagnosis and set support systems in

Chapter 1

motion. Denial was simple, welcome, understandable. It was Dad's coping mechanism, and we partially colluded with him in it.

We noticed the slow loss of faculties: deterioration in personal organisation, loss of ability to understand dates and times, hardness of hearing and forgetfulness. On one occasion I received a call out of the blue: 'We've got your dad's passport!' I was dumbfounded. It was the local cinema calling me to advise that they had found Dad's passport and a few other possessions in a carrier bag in their gents' toilet. I swung by there several days later to retrieve them, thinking, 'Aha, I've got some evidence now to show him that he needs to keep on top of things.' When I arrived at his house and delivered my sermon entitled, 'Dad—you need to be more careful,' he went into a meltdown of confusion, vulnerability, stammering and general lostness. My message was completely inappropriate and unwisely delivered.

He started needing more help with the telephone, as he struggled with phone numbers. I went and purchased a large button phone and programmed in the important numbers with photos next to them. Conversations on the phone became more difficult.

He struggled with being given directions. He went out on his own and wouldn't reappear, despite frantic calls to his mobile (which he never mastered how to use). He did, however, insist on having a smartphone, so we used that to our advantage by installing an app on it so that we could track the location of the phone (and hopefully its owner when he remembered to take it with him …).

Despite this, he managed to travel independently into London to meet me for a lunchtime sandwich in those early days, something I now treasure as a special time. But the decline continued, and it entailed my making more and more contact with his neighbours, who thankfully kept a look-out for him.

He lost the ability to ride a bike (a great personal loss, as he was a keen cyclist, having a number of bikes in his garage). He would

Disease development

frequently not put the phone back on the receiver, resulting in our contacting neighbours who would discreetly pop round to put it right. Additionally, he would regularly press the wrong button on the TV remote, rendering it useless, until (again) a neighbour would go round and restore it at press of a single button, much to Dad's incredulity: 'How did you do that?!' Dad in his earlier life had been a keen motorcyclist and, with the loss of the car, kept threatening to go and buy a moped/scooter. Needless to say, this was something we did our best to dissuade him from, hoping (and relying) on the savvy, if not the kindness, of the dealers not to sell him one.

Driverless (or autonomous cars), just over the horizon, were sadly not advanced enough in their development for Dad. A trial was taking place in Milton Keynes (where else?!), but to be a test user you had to be able to take over the running of the vehicle manually should an incident occur.

In fairness to Milton Keynes, it did come to the rescue, however, in the next development. Realising I was starting to be overwhelmed with care demands and not having a clue where to go for help, I reasoned that the best thing was to go and talk to someone. There was a plethora of information out there and it was completely confusing; I just wanted someone to answer a few questions and, more importantly, start to point me in the right direction. So, I contacted the Alzheimer's Society in Milton Keynes for an hour's free consultation. I was hesitant about what information they would give me, but was becoming increasingly aware that things were starting to slide and I needed to be on the front foot.

The meeting didn't start well. Coming from my own corporate, slick, pressurised work environment, I was brought up short by the counsellor walking in with a very casual and relaxed manner. However, the next hour proved definitive in Dad's care; I trace many subsequent blessings back to that one hour.

Calmly, it was explained to me that:

Chapter 1

- As Dad's ability to cope diminishes, the local authority will want to keep Dad in his own home for as long as possible.

- Attendance Allowance should be applied for, a non-means tested government financial assistance to vulnerable people.

- Care Plan—we were to discuss with the person living with dementia what their end-of-life care plan wants to look like, so that we could ensure their wishes are known and can be put in place.

- Care agencies and support services—funded care is available if you have less than £23,250 of cash or investment assets. There is nothing to stop you sourcing local care as and when it is needed, through private care agencies.

It was ground-breaking and felt like a weight had lifted from my shoulders, as I now had a sense of purpose and direction and knew that there was help out there. None of these steps were taken in the immediate weeks that followed, but some of the mental strain and loneliness was lifted and the cloud of unknowing was somewhat dispersed.

In everything Dad continued to resist all offers of help, so it became a war of attrition as we wore Dad down to accept help. Through it all the emphasis was on his being helped, on stress being removed, on making him less anxious, and on our being helped.

As he had lived alone for many years, we'd grown accustomed to his house being a bit of mess, but always excused it as part of who he was. He was organised, it was clean, and he was always on time. Yet increasingly he struggled to keep on top of keeping things in check. Early on I decided a cleaner would be a good idea, just to keep on top of things and ensure that he was safe and the

Disease development

house fit for dwelling. Age UK offered a domestic cleaner service, whereby they would send someone to the house to assess what was needed and agree with you what to do and how regularly. As a large charity, they were not in it to make a profit. They simply want to cover costs and provide a service to the vulnerable. At the same time, they'd loosely keep a check on the person when visiting and let you know if anything was untoward. Although Dad initially had the wherewithal to cancel the first appointment (which he did!) I managed to press ahead (several months later) and he eventually settled on a man coming once a week, then later a woman—both of whom quickly established themselves as friends of Dad. Their visits provided vital reassurance, as well as some company for Dad. Plus, we knew his house was habitable.

Similarly, after a period of time we realised that Dad, on his own much of the week, was becoming unable to use the oven or microwave—despite people explaining things on the phone to him. Increasingly, neighbours were stepping in to arrange meals for him; this was lovely in itself but an unreasonable expectation for us to keep laying on them. And it became a problem when the neighbours were away. So, we sourced a local domestic meals delivery service and started, on a few select days, to have some dinners (lunches) delivered. This later expanded to evening meals as well. Dad, being unable to process a menu, had to accept what we'd chosen. (We had made careful note of the senior generational issue of no spicy food, onions, etc., etc.) Thankfully, the meal delivery service knew their target audience, as spotted dick and custard was on the menu!

After the initial diagnosis there were several follow-up appointments with the specialist memory clinic to assess his needs and then discuss medication or treatment. Dad again was reluctant to go, and never mentioned the D word. On one of these visits, the doctor suggested his taking a low level early stage dementia medicine. He stated these were able to redress the effects of the

Chapter 1

disease, but then backtracked when I suggested that dementia medicine only held the symptoms at bay. Dad said it wasn't needed anyway, as he'd never needed any medicines in all his life, proudly boasting he was the only 80-year-old he knew who was not being kept going by a cocktail of pills and lotions. It wasn't helped by the fact that this was the doctor who had diagnosed Dad in the first place and been the one who had removed Dad's driving licence.

After one frosty and fruitless session, I drove Dad home in silence after he'd again refused medicines. While I was silently trying to hold back waves of anger (at him) and despair (at the seeming hopelessness of it all) Dad spoke up in the car: 'You think I'm making a mistake, don't you?'

I had to jump straight in at the opportunity but go at it subtly, from the side, in a disarming manner. 'I'm not sure you've much to lose, Dad.'

Eventually, after several of these visits, we managed to wear him down into taking the medicines. When he took the leaflet in his hand and noted the side effects … no, he wasn't having any of that. I then tried the 'What have you got to lose?' approach again. At yet another session he finally consented and agreed to be started on the lowest dose possible. I chose to capitalise immediately by going straight to the chemist and getting the medicine for him.

We then had a tricky issue to navigate. How could we ensure that Dad, living on his own, was going to commit and remember to take the pills? Discreetly, his partner and I put up an encouraging wall of observation around him to monitor his daily routines. By a process of slipping the subject innocuously into conversations we were able to ensure a reasonable strike rate in his actually taking the medicines. To help with him remembering (and to give us some evidence that he'd taken them) we procured a pill counter box, so that each morning and evening tablets could be visibly dispensed.

Disease development

Sadly, after several months Dad started to suffer some of the side effects, including have sudden toilet moments. The loss of dignity in public places was very difficult for him to bear. I realised, too, that a life of not taking any medicines meant he had a heightened sensitivity to any form of artificial chemicals and was therefore especially vulnerable to the side effects. We stopped the medicine, and after yet more visits to the doctor were able to start him on an alternative form. Sadly, these too resulted in more unpleasant side effects and this medicine was also dropped. From then on Dad took no further dementia medicines. This worry constantly gnawed away at me, knowing that nothing was in place to slow the headlong decline. Dad was utterly reliant on his own physical strength and conditioning to fight the disease. We'd used up any good will in persuading him to take medicines and quietly handed ourselves and Dad over to succumb to the disease.

Much is written about taking the positive mental approach in dealing with dementia. Rather than saying someone *has* dementia (and therefore creating a victim mentality) the Alzheimer's Society encourage people to adopt the approach of saying that someone is *living with* dementia. We tried that positive approach, especially when mentioning it to other people. Dad, however, continued to refuse to say there was anything wrong and continued not to say he was unwell. He fought bravely and with dignity.

As Dad declined in an unchecked manner, we noticed there were long periods where we observed little change: he would continue to cope with life and its challenges at about the same level. Then suddenly, we'd notice that it had not been such a good visit, where he'd struggled with something new. His decline seemed to plateau and then drop suddenly to a diminished level. There was never any actual improvement, although he did learn to cope with his lessening abilities.

Chapter 1

Worrying about what the future might hold, I started drip-feeding into conversations about arranging power of attorney, although I had no idea about what this entailed. Dad refused to speak about it, fearing we'd take over his money and home. In a war of attrition, I decided my best tactic was to overwhelm him by demonstrating our care for him. Every weekend I would be down at his house, cleaning it, sorting furniture, bikes, garden, and the like. Meanwhile, I got hold from the government website the form and guide on completing lasting of powers of attorney (there are two: finances and health; I chose to concentrate on finances first). Eventually, over several months I completed the form and lined up a kindly neighbour of Dad's to be the witness. There were several aborted attempts to get him to sign it ('Not today,' 'Let's do it next weekend,' etc.), before we finally sat down with his neighbour. Even then Dad was reluctant to sign, and in the end she saved the day, persuading him to sign, explaining she'd done the same already with her own sons. Once it was signed (with my breathing a huge sigh of relief) I then had it witnessed myself, passed it to my sister to do likewise before sending it off to the government department. Twelve weeks later it returned, completed and ready to be put into place.

I repeated the whole process again for the health power of attorney when his mental and physical abilities were starting seriously to be eroded. As it turned out, this one was never required. No agency or solicitors were needed to be involved, as it can be self-processed. Once each was in place, I found a local solicitor to make certified copies. The Financial LPA needed several versions (for banks, solicitors, savings, care homes and the like).

Unaware of what the slow decline would be like, we continued on with holidays as per normal. It became clear, however, that Dad's ability to cope with long days, travel, unfamiliar routes and food quickly diminished. A team of people were needed to surround him while going to familiar places. Dad, of course, was unaware of the

Disease development

level of work and effort going on around him, so he could enjoy the simple pleasures of an ice cream on the beach. In 2016 Dad went camping with the family, and again in 2017, but it became much more of a strain, especially on his partner. Typically, if caring for him we'd have to build in considerable enabling time to get Dad up, washed, dressed, fed, and ready to step out of the door. It became similar to looking after a child, though recognising him as a full adult, with developed feelings, thoughts and emotions. It was necessary to consider before leaving the house what things he'd need during the day (spare items of personal clothing, glasses, medicines, money, cards, keys, etc.). We were having to do the thinking for him.

A life-long aspiration of Dad's was to travel on some of the Swiss railways, and he'd mentioned it a number of times over the years without ever getting around to sorting it. Having got power of financial attorney and starting to wrestle with his various bank accounts and savings, I realised there were little pots of money squirrelled away in many places; it certainly wasn't an affordability issue that had held Dad back. As Dad was too vulnerable and incapable of the relatively independent travel that being part of a tour group entails (there was no way he could reliably process 'Be on platform 4 in 20 minutes,' when at Geneva Station), I wondered if I could go with him as his carer. Discussing this with my wife, we agreed this would be a great once-in-a-lifetime trip for father and son, sharing a week's train travel and hoteling in Switzerland. I went ahead and booked for the two of us to go. Although I'd have the company of Dad, he would be utterly reliant on me to consider and arrange his needs, as it would be unfair to rely on the other holidaymakers in the group, or the tour guide, to watch out for him. Realising this would potentially be a lonely trip I then decided to take my own son (who was 10 at the time) out of school for the trip as well, as additional company and help for both me and Dad. To

Chapter 1

my surprise, when emailing the school about taking my son out for a week, they were commendably broad-minded about it, responding with a 'We can't approve the absence but it sounds like a great trip—have a great time!'

We travelled by TGV through to Geneva, then local trains to the hotel, where we arrived well after dark, exhausted after an exceptionally long day. Dad coped ever so well. Throwing open the curtains the next morning we were greeted by the most spectacular vista of stunning blue sky and lofty, grand mountains and craggy ridges, framed with golden autumnal colours of trees on the turn. It really was as though God had laid out the very best for us.

The weather stayed glorious all week, with sunny clear skies and temperate conditions so we could enjoy day trips to Montreux, Chamonix and the Matterhorn, all on local Swiss trains. All three of us loved it, and I was so utterly grateful we were given this window of safety to enjoy the wonderful beauty of Switzerland, its people, trains and hospitality. Dad particularly enjoyed the trains all day and then jumping in the swimming pool before dinner, followed by a glass of wine in the bar. Truly it was a gift from the Lord. Take whatever life holidays you've wanted to do and get them done while you can. There were incidents along the way and it wasn't plain sailing. I particularly found it exhausting doing all the thinking for the three of us. Dad just about coped overall and we just about got away with it. A couple of months later and it would not have been possible.

As life continued to be more and more of a struggle for Dad, we noticed that dressing, eating, walking and following simple instructions became more challenging and took longer and longer. He became more tired and would doze more frequently, limiting our ability as to what we could do as a family.

We started having family meetings behind his back, discussing what we needed to do for him (lifts, day visits, key safes being

Disease development

installed, and so on). I set up a family WhatsApp group, so we could co-ordinate what was going on.

Tackling more serious issues (that we had kept sweeping under the carpet) meant making enquiries about whether Dad had a will. None of this was volunteered by him. After considerable chasing and enquiring it turned out his will resided at an old family firm of solicitors. They wouldn't release the will to Dad or to us, and in fact this ended up as a running sore until after Dad's passing.

Dad started to regress in his life memories. He sometimes could not recall life details, but then when we were out for a meal one evening he launched into episodes of his early adult life that I'd previously never heard him discussing: National Service in the RAF and the like. We started collating photo albums for him in order to help trigger memories and so to help him remember who he was and who his family was before the memories slipped away.

The increasing burden of care for Dad started to really impact and manifest itself on my family—constantly caring for Dad and discussing him with my wife and children meant he dominated the landscape. Many weekends were given over to helping Dad, installing furniture, making his house safer, giving lifts, doing chores for him, stuff to the tip, meetings with care helpers....

It became an exercise in delicately weaving our way through family meetings to resolve matters. The WhatsApp group took on a life of its own, with some occasional unhelpful comments providing sources of anger and frustration. Eventually my wife came off the group as she found it unhelpful. We struggled sometimes to get agreement on some matters; always the focus kept coming back to what was best for Dad. We started having the longer-range conversations about a strategy for moving Dad into care (or getting more home care help). I raised the issue with Dad on a few occasions when it seemed prudent, but on each occasion it was clear he didn't understand or couldn't articulate his views or concerns. My message

Chapter 1

back to him, when positioning the arguments for more care, revolved around some familiar themes: 'You're not coping, Dad; move closer to us; make your life easier; we're doing the worrying for you; your care requirements are not fair on neighbours; think of all the things you'll still be able to do, etc., etc.'

The impact of all the additional driving and expenses started to mount up—we purchased a cheap run-about second car, in part so as to free up one of us to run Dad about at weekends. Petrol costs increased, as did the food bill. Many of the weekends involved fitting in around Dad or taking him out for meals. He no longer functioned as 'Dad' or 'Partner' and became a dependant, all the while thinking he was still independent.

Eventually, I was able to register the previously arranged financial power of attorney with his two main banks, get duplicate cards issued and started to take over the management of his finances. This involved spending considerable time down at his house wrestling with his out-of-control filing system—he'd been organised and had regular financial check-ups, but things had gotten on top of him and I was presented with a fairly chaotic picture of bank statements squirrelled away all over the place, stuffed into drawers and mixed up.

I registered for online banking and started paying trades, carer agencies, supporting organisations. A wise friend said that you should adopt the principles of how Dad used to be and repeat that: namely if he was generous or would help people (from family help or paying for coffees) then do likewise.

We put in place some other straightforward practical helps: I had several sets of duplicate keys made and distributed these around the family, and purchased and installed a key safe by the front door; we discreetly re-jigged furniture and removed a number of trip hazards (done one by one over a number of visits so it wasn't noticeable).

Disease development

Nonetheless, matters were coming to a head. Dad increasingly couldn't be left on his own for long periods. He started to lose the ability to dress himself, do simple personal hygiene, prepare meals for himself, or remember doctor's appointments. The fire brigade ended up round at Dad's twice, once after his microwave caught fire and once after locking himself out. Ditto, the police visited after he'd gone walkabout. Neighbours were completely and unreasonably relied upon to look out for him. On one occasion, he'd visited one of them no fewer than six times by 12:30 lunchtime! Clearly things were moving to a crisis and we concluded that external help was needed.

After some difficult conversations where I laid the groundwork with Dad that he needed help, we managed to source meals being delivered a few times a week (lunches at first and then, later, evening meals). We also sourced a morning carer for an hour a morning during the week when Dad was waking up alone. They got Dad up, washed, dressed and breakfasted, so as to help him start the day. He increasingly would then go straight round to a neighbour's. He couldn't cope being alone and couldn't face the vacuum of an empty day. Later we moved to having evening carers come round to repeat the process. All of this Dad resisted, not able to understand why it was needed. It meant quite an adjustment, knowing a relative stranger was there in the house with him. The loss of dignity was considerable. He couldn't comprehend why he was going to bed early, but with the carers we had got it was the only way we could make it work.

After some months of making do, juggling meals, carers, cleaners and the like we reached the conclusion that Dad needed permanent, 24-hour care. We debated long on whether to get Dad move in with us, but several people advised against it. My wife considered giving up work, but there were levels of discomfort and sacrifice associated with this, plus we were told it would impose considerable strain on the home situation. I knew Dad would have straightaway said yes

Chapter 1

if we had asked him to move in with us. Eventually we considered a local care home, made visits several times, got others in the family to do the same, went through paperwork with them and took the plunge to move Dad there. Before committing, I took Dad there for a visit—he blew up with rage afterwards, shouting at me and the kids in Costa when I took him there for a 'What do you think?' conversation.

We left it for a while to simmer down a bit, but knew it was a temporary respite; his care needs were too great. We were circling around the confrontation and hoped Dad would come to the realisation that he needed full-time care. What we couldn't appreciate was that his ability to reason and work that through was gone; he had no capacity to join the dots as such. Two months later we were back again at the care home, visiting with Dad and discussing behind the scenes a room and moving-in date.

We persisted, in the end involving Social Services (pleading with them). They came round to visit, together with a close and helpful neighbour, and he reluctantly, arguing and grumbling, consented to Social Services' insistence that he needed to move into care. He sat there, head in hands, overwhelmed at being confronted with evidence against him (being out in the street at 10pm, the police view, the strain on neighbours, etc., etc.).

By this stage the care home had become seared into his consciousness, however, and he was resistant to going, not wanting the move, while they were reluctant to take him in as a resident in such circumstances. At the last moment we reached a true crisis point. It was obvious from Dad's reactions he was aware of the enforced change and was desperately angry at moving into care. The tension was palpable. I was down on my knees crying to God: 'I don't know what to do!' In desperation my wife started making phone calls one Sunday morning (we'd skipped church) and by the end of the day had sourced a full-time live-in carer through

Disease development

a care agency. The carer was due to go somewhere and start a residency, but at the last moment it had fallen through, so was now unexpectedly available at short notice (providence!). We agreed a moving-in date of the Tuesday, and as it happened I was off work that week (providence again!) and so was able on the Sunday to order all the additional furniture he'd need (bed, mattress, etc.), and then on the Monday/Tuesday clear out a bedroom and install the furniture in Dad's house. On the Tuesday afternoon this stranger arrived (we'd skimmed a resumé, no photo) to start a full-time live-in care arrangement with Dad. He took Dad off for a walk while I went through the paperwork with the care agency manager, advising them on Dad's preferences and requirements. After some hesitation and nervousness all round we then left Dad and his carer together to get to know one another.

The carer was very gentle with Dad and his needs, patient, tolerant and yet firm when needed if Dad was being unreasonable. The agency said that every four to six weeks a new carer would be swapped in—a potential nightmare of starting again and confusion for Dad, who desperately needed stability. We'd been told, if you get a good carer then stick with them. Thankfully (providence, yet again!) this carer was happy to stay in the post long term and ended up being in situ for almost five months.

We did have to make a number of structural changes in the house: better, more suitable furniture (wing-back chair anyone?), moving stuff around, de-cluttering, simplifying layouts of rooms, taking keys off dad and the like. To keep things stable and routine for Dad we agreed for him to continue his weekend stays at his partner's house and our house, thereby giving the carer much-needed breaks. At the same time, we arranged a bank card for him and agreed on the management of a cash float, as we effectively had to hand over the daily management of Dad to the carer, entrusting him entirely with Dad's welfare. Later, considering all the taxi and bus

Chapter 1

fares, I sorted out car insurance and handed over our second car to the carer, to be able to run Dad about more independently (and consequently free up the family from some of the running about). Retrospectively I wish I'd done this sooner, as it was a great benefit to Dad, his carer and the family.

Despite Dad now being under the watchful eye of a full-time carer, he would still slip out the house in unguarded moments when, say, the carer was taking a shower. Dad would be found round at the usual neighbour's, wondering what was going on or seeking some assurance. It was heart-breaking to watch his decline into a child-like state, from being a confident, informed, helpful, outgoing, gracious man. He had moments of being unsafe in public and at home. This continued to be unfair on neighbours and placed further strain on the family. Living with a full-time carer, in itself a God-send, did, however, allow for a more structured life for Dad and he was more settled and content. We roped in support from the NHS Support services teams, to install handrails and provide occupational and mental health support.

After five months of full-time live-in care, we could see Dad getting noticeably weaker and more confused, despite the constant care and life being arranged around him. He was able to go on some simple holidays to Dorset and Norfolk (we had to say no to a family scheme for him to go to Barcelona on a budget airline flight, as there was no way he would have withstood the rigours of air travel). People started to say that he needed to be in a full-time care facility; he couldn't manage the stairs in his own home; he made the statement, 'I feel sad'; he was noticeably more tired; he sounded so distant on the phone and was aware that he was losing the battle. Once again we started to explore and worry about our options. We looked at making structural changes in his house (moving bedrooms and bathrooms around, getting more carers in to help, etc., as he could no longer safely manage the stairs). Once again, we examined

Disease development

the idea of moving Dad to our own family home but came back to the same conclusion that it would be too much upheaval. Sadly, it was also far too late in his decline for him to be able to cope.

Having concluded that the previous care home had become 'toxic' in his mind-set (and that they were reluctant to take him, steering us down the Deprivation of Liberty route, involving Social Services), we started to look around and I went on the Care Quality Commission website and did a simple search in care homes radiating out from our postcode. Sifting the results, on a (providentially!) rare weekend free of Dad and kids responsibilities, we were able at short notice to arrange a visit. On arriving with my wife, walking inside I immediately thought, 'Oohh no!' Yet, after walking around, talking with staff and seeing his potential room, in the course of an hour I had completely changed my mind, as had my wife. This place did not feel like an institution, but more like a 1950's B and B—high ceilings, light and airy, gloss white woodwork, old fashioned wallpaper, yet clean and comfortable, with a lovely garden and caring staff.

We arranged for other members of the family to visit while liaising with Dad's carer to transition Dad across. We considered a temporary week there, as respite, but concluded it needed to be a straight move. At church the next morning I casually turned to an elderly couple behind us and they enquired about my Dad. Off the bat they said, 'It's a lovely care home; we've had two aunts stay there.' God, it seems, was moving the pieces together and making a way for us. The room was available, it met all criteria and was close by. We arranged relatively easily for the room to be refreshed and agreed a move-in date. Sadly, before that could happen, Dad was taken seriously ill while we were away in Devon—he was in intensive care with pneumonia and only just pulled through. We moved him straight from hospital to the residential care home. Sadly again, he was there for only three weeks before passing away, surrounded by his family. The care home allowed us all the freedom,

Chapter 1

overnight stays and help we needed to allow us to be there, present, for Dad in his last days. They were the model of what a care home should be. Dad was given dignity, love, safety and all the care he needed, as were we, before his passing.

Chapter 2

External help

It is important to realise that you cannot possibly hope to manage the care of someone with dementia on your own, whatever form it takes. The scale of the care issues placed on you will be considerable, not to mention the amount of life decisions you will need to make on behalf of someone. On top of that there is a bewildering array of potential help out there … but the knowledge of that and lack of clear guidance compounds the anguish. And there is a need for you to seek help for yourself and your family and friends all caring for the person with dementia.

Here are some of the organisations we used, that you might find helpful:

1. The Alzheimer's Society

Nearly two years into Dad's diagnosis the sense of creeping worry could no longer be put off—I was desperate for someone to make head and tail of it all, to bounce thoughts off and to get some simple signposting. As a charity, the Alzheimer's Society's advice was a priceless and timely intervention. Make contact and have a session with them for help. They gave a raft of advice, much of it repeated here, from fundamental steps such as putting in place an Advanced Care Plan (templates online) to simple measures such as a memory card to be inserted in his wallet.

Chapter 2

2. NHS—End of Life Care Plan

Online forms help capture your thoughts on end of life care. They facilitate the conversations, ensuring wishes are known, documented and can be put into place when the time comes and when the person living with the dementia no longer has capacity to articulate their preferences. It also saves later family arguments on funeral arrangements.

3. Attendance Allowance

As care demands increase, through more visits, lifts, care services, meals, home helps, and so on, there is considerable strain placed on the finances of the person with dementia and the family and friends. For such the government offers non-means-tested financial support to help with those needs. The form is online and can be relatively easily completed. Twelve weeks following completion of this form a letter of confirmation was received, and funds started dropping into Dad's bank account on a monthly basis. There is no scrutiny on how it is spent: it is given to assist with care demands as you see fit. There are lower and higher amounts of financial assistance given, backdated to when the demands increased. I was advised to complete the form on the basis of what a bad day for Dad looked like.

4. Care funding

Care for individuals falls to the local authority in its various guises, and as such this can include a variety of care services tailored to the person's particular needs. In the UK the philosophy is for those in need to remain in their own homes for as long as possible, so as to be comfortable and in their own surroundings. This way, too, they are not a burden on the over-stretched care system. Should the person in need have personal funds over £23,250 then they will be required to fund their own care, either through personally procured private

External help

care services or by voluntarily moving into a care home, self-funded. It should be stressed there are ambiguities in this approach (such as what happens if a person moves into an expensive privately funded care home and then runs out of funds). Local authorities are aware of games and tricks that people can play to hide funds in order to receive state funded care; I even heard of local authorities employing private detectives to investigate cases where they had suspicions of malpractice or deceit.

Dad had sufficient savings and so this meant he bore the cost of his personal care. It was pointed out to me by a trusted friend that a useful outlook to take might be that 'it his money for his personal care, and his careful, prudent lifestyle had made provision for that'. Additionally, due to his saving, he (and the family) were then able to pick and choose his care, tailoring it to his individual tastes and needs; he was not at the mercy of the local authority sending him to a care facility not of his choosing. Dad was in a relatively blessed position to do this; not everyone is able to have this privilege.

5. Council tax rebate

Local authorities will grant 25% discounts off Council Tax rates for single occupancy dwelling—Dad already had this in place. However, I discovered that it is possible to have this zero-rated if the person has proven and significant needs of care. Again, an online local form needs to be completed with the local authority. Eventually this was completed and the Council provided a rebate stretching back to the point Dad's needs had escalated.

6. Register with Social Services

After some considerable investigation (and as had been highlighted by Alzheimer's Society) I concluded that Social Services needed to become involved in Dad's care; in fact, it became vital to be on their radar, to be visited, assessed (as an Assessment of Need) and have a

Chapter 2

care plan in place. They have the legal powers and responsibility to ensure adequate care is in place. Again, as another seriously overstretched local resource, it paid to be continuously very persistent with them, politely hounding them to get involved, rather than waiting for the system to catch up. I had to escalate matters to a supervisor to get a visit, and then again subsequently when Dad's needs were desperate. They suggested it be remedied with one or two more day-time care visits whereas he urgently needed to be in 24-hour care at that point. Only after my pointing that out on the phone in stark and unequivocal terms did they react and come straight back round to Dad's in order to take the lead on getting him to agree to move into care. They are the professionals in this situation.

7. Local care and memory groups and day centres

Find out who these are and start taking your loved one living with dementia to these—the local authority will have details of who these are. The social interaction and stimulus are a real tonic and it gives you and your relative something good to look forward to and a change of scene.

Chapter 3

Practical steps

Looking after a person living with dementia is a worrying and stressful ordeal, with a tendency to catch you out on practical details. The following is a summary of some of the practical steps we took to make Dad's life easier and safer and to help us in the running of his home and meeting his care needs:

- **Take hold of passports**—discreetly remove these, so as to prevent loss and also in case these are needed for trips. Do the same with European Health cards.

- **Get lots of spare keys cut**—distribute these out round family, friends, neighbours and carers. Have duplicates on your own house key sets and those of your car(s), as you may travel with the same keys each time.

- **Fit a key safe** and memorise the access code—useful for service providers such as carers, cleaners, meal providers, neighbours, tradespeople, etc.

- **Consider using a GPS tracker** or have a suitable (free) app installed on their phone and yours—you will be able to see where the person is when they go AWOL. There are key fobs that provide a similar service.

Chapter 3

- **Do household practical things**—replace light bulbs, remove carpet mats that may be trip hazards, make the house gas safe (we removed the gas fire through our own safety concerns and then replaced the microwave after Dad set fire to the old one and the big red lorry turned up!)

- **Buy the person easier clothes** to get into and out of. The days of high fashion have gone, and it will be time to make way for comfortable and practical clothing.

- **Consider professional services**, either privately, if funds permit, or enrol them through Social Services. We reached a crisis point of neighbours repeatedly texting me about Dad's whereabouts and welfare, which forced us to intervene and arrange morning care visits. This involved Dad shouting down the phone at me that he did not need care when in fact he desperately did and couldn't see it. Involve and include the neighbours, family and friends in this as needed. Prepare yourself before the conversations so as to remain calm and reasoned when explaining the care needs.

- **Home help**—consider getting a gardener in to take over some the practical care of the garden maintenance—again it relieves the strain from their lives and feelings of not coping.

- **Post**—consider getting it redirected to your own home, as again it becomes a source of stress to the person living with dementia. As much as possible it is about removing the layers of responsibility in the person's life, as it becomes something else they can't cope with or understand. Alternatively, if they cannot accept it, then ask them to set the post aside—this will necessitate you (or others) visiting regularly in order to handle it. Similarly, get on top of their filing and accounts systems—in my case I eventually removed Dad's filing cabinets to my own home in order to manage his finances, utilities, etc. more efficiently.

- **Friends and neighbours**—may or may not pick up some of the localised responsibilities as their situation makes them more aware of what's going on. This actually became an additional worry, for they were over-reaching themselves in their good endeavours, love and care—I had to keep checking that they were all right with being voluntarily so involved. Keep close to those who are critically involved in the support of the person needing care and agree, even loosely, with what they are doing and note what they say you need to be aware of. I frequently had to engineer conversations with them out of sight of Dad—thank goodness for text messaging! Watch out for relationships ebbing and flowing a bit. When Dad fell out with them, thankfully they were all compassionate and understood it was the disease that caused moments of anger to flare up. Their love and care were exemplary as they graciously acknowledged that it was not the old Dad. Similarly, become reliant on a network of local tradespeople to undertake maintenance works as needed.

- **Tell your boss**, as they have a duty of care. Explore opportunities to work from home, or work from your relative's house—you'd be surprised who else has been through it. Work colleagues had a lot of advice and support.

- **Recruit a financial advisor.** They can help you manage assets on behalf of those you are caring for and can give advice on care funding and support; they can also remove some of the administrative strain.

- **Delegate tasks to neighbours, friends and family** as much as you are able to, so as to spread the load. You cannot take on the herculean task of 24/7 care for one person. As Dad declined, his level of care and support rose considerably, as it became necessary to do more of the thinking for him. Keep an eye on the delegation, however, to make sure you give clear instructions and that tasks are getting completed. They are not doing a favour for you, rather helping to care for a needy individual. Don't make it personal to you or use it to settle (or open up) family grievances. You all need to be pulling in the same direction. Make peace with the fact that for various reasons some elements of your family won't be involved. That in itself can be a tremendous source of frustration, but you have to deal with yourself, almost boxing off the irritation, as you need to focus on the care. Issues and grievances can be addressed later where needed.

- **Keep the lines of communication open** with family and friends and prepare yourself for disagreements as to what the person can and cannot do; you won't have all the answers.

- **Get Social Services involved**—register with them via the local authority. Do it as soon as you can, regardless of how the person is coping or their financial means to support themselves. You need to be on their radar as they have the legal duty of care over the person who needs it and you need to form a working relationship with the appointed social worker.

- **See the person's GP**, so that you know them, and have phone numbers stored. Establish their medical history, get a working and trusted relationship going with the doctor and support staff at the local surgery. The GP can call in support from local occupational health professionals in order to help with practical arrangements in the home (handrails, door sensors, etc.).

Practical steps

- **Consider moving the person closer to you** while they have the capability to do so and are able to cope with the change.

- **Stress the benefits of all you are doing** for the person—they will have limited ability to appreciate it, but nonetheless it helps them possibly make sense in even a limited way of what is going on. Reinforce that there is a team of folks who are loving and caring for them.

- **Utilise the Care Quality Commission's register** of care providers. Make appointments and go and visit them, asking searching questions about their services. Read the latest inspection reports. Encourage the person to visit for short respite periods, to establish familiarity and to give you a break. It will help with the later transitioning to full time care, if and when needed.

- **Finally, most crucially, covet the prayers** of your family, friends, support groups and church—you will need to be upheld in the care process. God knows and will work for those who wait for Him (Isaiah 64:4).

Chapter 4

Dealing with yourself

As the call on your time, energy and resources increases, the most important person to care for is yourself. The strain on your ability to make practical, clear-minded decisions and interventions will increase as time and the condition progress. You will need to remain on top form in order to maximise your effectiveness, and there is a need to recognise that this diminishes as you come under added pressure, just when the decisions get more critical. Prepare yourself for a battle, long term. You are in this potentially for the long haul. It may be a cliché, but it's definitely true: it is a marathon, not a sprint, and so it is important to pace yourself and look after your own mental, physical and spiritual health.

During the development of the person's dementia, you yourself will increasingly also be a sufferer as you deal with the consequences. Recognise that you will have to deal with a whole range of emotions, often at times of weakness or when you are not expecting them. Let's consider some of the primary ones that are likely to arise:

Anger. You will have people get angry at you, including the person living with dementia, often when it's understandable, often when it's not. Remember, it is the disease manifesting itself through or in the person. Recognise too that others will get angry with you. And you will get angry with yourself for making mistakes. Be kind to yourself. But also allow yourself to be angry—it is a disease, it is a robbing of their dignity and capacity; it is wrong, it wasn't meant to be like this. Yes, it feels unfair and lonely; be angry that some of your life is on hold (for now).

Dealing with yourself

Tiredness. You are not superhuman, and during the care and strain you will have even less energy than usual, in part due to the worry and constant stress. Try to get regular sleep to give yourself a fitting chance of at least keeping the wheels turning.

Self-pity. There will be a tendency for events and the weight of responsibility to fall heavily upon you. In such circumstances, when in a crucible of testing, we can succumb to default behaviours and our weaknesses and sub-optimal responses tend to surface—be prepared for bouts of self-pity and feeling maudlin. Recognise what is going on in yourself and allow yourself some slack, but don't let it become an excuse for despondency or giving up. People are relying on you. Make yourself accountable to others and seek their help to lift you up. Find legitimate (non-addictive) outlets for your emotions.

Weight gain/loss. One default response is comfort eating, especially late at night when the rush and stress of the day subsides. Waves of anxiety can find you propping open the fridge door and swilling a glass of wine. On the other hand, weight loss through stressing and forgetting to eat may lead to further tiredness and lower your ability to cope, just when you need to be on your A-game.

Exercise. As over-eating (or at least comfort eating) establishes itself, there is similarly less desire to find available time to exercise, again, just when you most need sharp personal energy levels. Try to make exercise something you do with someone else (such as arranging a squash match or bike ride with a mate) as it is harder to pull out of that.

Sleep. We all go through periods of no or little sleep. However, with the stress of coping with a person living with dementia the worry is sufficient to cause sleepless anxiety, exacerbated by the additional things to do that lead to later nights and earlier mornings. Do the small obvious things to help yourself: less bingeing, caffeinated drinks and alcohol and screen time towards the end of the evening.

Chapter 4

Having a recharging night's sleep sets you up to be able to cope better with the demands on your time, heart and emotions.

Give up stuff. Time will be limited and you will find that you cannot maintain a diverse and full life of activities that you may have previously enjoyed. Now is a time and season to focus on the priorities. Some things you thought important will naturally fall by the wayside. Balance that with the need to do normal stuff occasionally: go to a football match, meet up with a mate for a curry, go for a run, or whatever, to try and maintain some sort of normality.

Retail. Financial commitments may mean that this is not an option, and indeed the increased care may mean there is less time available for any sort of retail therapy. Additionally, funds may not permit this as you are spending much of your spare financial resources in helping to carry for others. Plus, the desire to shop may diminish as you realise in the overall scheme of things it is not important how you are dressed. Treat yourself as and when you may be able to, for sure, but don't let retail slake your thirst, as it is at best a temporary buzz and distraction.

Temptations. Other temptations may present themselves, dependent on your own predispositions and circumstances. Be generally aware of your thought life and try and put measures in place to guard yourself. Make yourself accountable to others.

Loss of friends. Previously important friendships may evaporate as you simply don't have time to focus on meeting up from time to time for banal chat and distractions. Only those who are truly your friends will continue to stand by your side.

Experiences. I personally found myself on YouTube at night, watching videos on motorbikes, dreaming of some sort of escape. Thankfully I was providentially held back from putting down a deposit on a new Fireblade—a good thing, as I was acutely aware that others were depending on me. Aside from the risk of letting

Dealing with yourself

things get out of control was the thought that I had no spare time to be riding it anyway, and thankfully I saw it for the distraction it was.

Be careful with whom you choose to be vulnerable. You will need emotional support from others, especially those closest to yourself, and there may be a temptation as you feel you can't cope to lean on others, some of whom aren't in your immediate circle of support. Be wary of who you tell what, as making yourself vulnerable to others with your burdens may make you vulnerable to forming emotional attachments and dependencies that could lead down some unwanted roads. Now may not be the time for a new relationship, although you may feel that's exactly what you need. Rarely does a relationship forged in the crucible of caring develop into a deep and foundational (or healthy) new relationship. Watch your thought life.

Desires and appetites are going to ebb and flow. Natural desires will wane, as you have less capacity to give of yourself. Your partner will know and support this, but do have the conversations to reassure them of where they stand with you (that this is just a season, etc.). You also will need reassurance yourself. As in some other aspects of your life it will create strain and it is important to recognise that. God will uphold you and keep you from temptation as faith takes hold of Him.

Concerning dealing with yourself, an essential question kept nagging away at me and repeatedly came to the surface: 'How can I believe in God if He's not going to save my Dad?!' Be honest. This is a make-or-break issue. Write down your thoughts and feelings. In the end I sought out a trusted, faithful and knowledgeable friend with this question. No direct answer was forthcoming, but I was at least allowed to articulate the full horror of what I was potentially facing. There is no room to sweep this under the carpet and I knew I needed to face it, or at least to know others were praying for me as I ministered in the last days. More of this later in the book.

Chapter 4

Ask your work colleagues to step up if you can. Tell your boss, as he/she has a duty of care for you and needs to be aware of what is going on in your life. You'll be surprised who else has been through these experiences and can offer a sympathetic ear.

Have difficult conversations early on or as soon as they are needed, both with your families and friends and with the person you are caring for. Set out your expectations for their behaviours and support. Remind them that the primary focus is the care of the person with dementia.

You will get through this. God will uphold you as you care, as you call on Him in your need. Faith plugs into His promises in Jesus—rely on Him as He sovereignly cares for you and the person you are looking after.

Don't lose sight of the fact that family matters and that they are going through this with you. Schedule a family break. In the midst of the strain as things were reaching a critical point in Dad's care, we took a break for a weekend in Poole—just for the chance to step away from the care and responsibility and to get some space and sunshine. People will be depending on you.

Finally, consider getting help around you, including care for the person with dementia and also for yourself. The carers need caring for. Swallow your pride and call out for help.

Reconcile yourself to needing more care help and that there will be strangers in your relative's house. Maybe they will move into your own family home—the quicker you can adapt and get used to it the better. Furniture will be moved around, personal space will diminish, as your world feels constrained and gets smaller. Retain your primary focus on the person you are caring for. The Lord will carry you through this: His grace is sufficient. To Him be the glory.

Chapter 5

Dealing with the person

As we've already seen, the onset of dementia in a person is a challenge to those around them and those especially tasked with dealing with their care. It is helpful to consider, though, the actual person themselves, those who are now living with the condition. It is easy to overlook that they are an actual person in their own right, with thoughts, feelings, emotions, as they battle the disease. For them, it is not an abstract condition, it's reality; they are ones facing the confusion, the loss of ability, the isolation and loneliness that dementia can often bring. Dealing with care is not just a strategy to be put into place. There is a human person, unique, gifted, precious, who is falling victim to this terrible disease, caught up in the middle of the loss and hurt. The question to consider is: How do we help them cope with it personally as their ability to communicate and process thoughts and ideas and their perception of the world round them is diminishing?

It is important to remember that their ability to rationalise, articulate and comprehend what is going on within themselves and to themselves will change as the condition develops. There will be many things that you will not be able to explain to them, while some matters can be communicated in basic terms at a level they can understand; this will need to be adapted to fit the person and their stage in the development of the disease.

Perhaps one of the most difficult (and early experienced) hurdles was the loss of independence that came from Dad losing his driving

Chapter 5

licence. For a formerly competent, independent and capable man, having his primary mode of transport taken away was a massive loss, experienced very early on in the diagnosis. Others depended on his being mobile and it required a change of expectation from them, but more so from Dad himself. He suddenly transitioned to needing lifts everywhere (not being comfortable with taxis), to getting the bus, and needing favours from family members. It was a blow to his confidence and a measure of his grace in the way he went about being reconciled to the loss. In hindsight, it was an unwelcome wake-up call for Dad and for us as a family.

Dad's memory continued to decline over a period, plateauing for long periods and then suddenly declining rapidly. He lost the ability to follow simple instructions, cook food for himself, dress himself and make decisions. Perhaps this loss of dignity, more than anything, was hardest for Dad to bear. Time and again he was put in compromising situations, needing help dressing, washing and going to the toilet which he struggled to cope with. There were awkward conversations at the doctor's that were embarrassing for him and were confusing for him to accept.

He became frustrated at times in not being able to articulate matters and understand others. His sense of loneliness increased as he became increasingly housebound and reliant on others for some structure to his day. He would go for walks just so as to be out meeting people, or because it was ingrained habit. As mentioned, on one occasion he knocked on a neighbour's door six times before 12:30 lunch time—out of pure habit and confusion. On another occasion, he presented a set of keys to the neighbour as he'd completely forgotten why he'd called round there.

Rumbling away in the back of Dad's consciousness was the fact that he knew on some level that things were getting serious—he could see, albeit on a limited level, that he was declining, although sadly he wasn't able (or brave enough) to articulate it. Peering into

Dealing with the person

his life, it was difficult to know what was going behind his eyes, but there was certainly some sort of awareness behind the scenes. It must have been worrying and saddening to be conscious of this. Emphasis was always placed on being in the moment, enjoying the here and now, keeping things light and positive, and on making decisions behind the scenes for him, removing the burden from his consciousness as much as possible.

Coupled with the awareness of the condition developing was the associated loss of dignity that went with it. Simple tasks like needing help with dressing and washing meant he was frequently put in compromising situations that were hard for a proud and respectable person to cope with. Added to that was the loss of memory, whereby he would struggle over words and the ability to communicate his wishes clearly; this all added to his despondency and frustration at times. Continuing erosion of decision making, and loss of awareness of circumstances and surroundings further stripped away his personality and character. Each time there was a loss of ability, it felt like a diminishing of the person he was, until Dad was reduced to a more child-like dependence, a shadow of who he had been. Yet despite these sad declines he remained in his core the same person with his cheery outlook, welcome smile and warm personality up until the very end of his days.

As Dad's abilities to make decisions became more hampered and he was unable to handle instructions, it became essential to frame decisions we wanted him to make in very simple, binary terms, so as to engender in him a sense of some sort of control and that he still had influence and purpose. Other practical steps were taken in the early days, such as sourcing a more user-friendly mobile phone, and making sure keys were with neighbours so he knew not to worry about home access. Additionally, in the early days it was still possible to have a conversation with Dad and tell him how things were making us feel about his condition. He could handle lower

Chapter 5

levels of emotional empathy for a while, although that receded with time. We were able to help Dad live well with dementia for most of the time, keeping his life positive, happy and straightforward, without his feeling closed in.

In dealing with the person, be self-aware that they will have bouts of anger and frustration and embarrassment. At times like these it was helpful to remember it was the disease causing these outbursts, not necessarily the old Dad as we knew him—it was helpful, so as to deflect the slight and hurt that we may have felt, as we were in the firing line from time to time. Prepare yourself for toilet episodes and arm yourself with the resources to maintain their dignity as much as possible. A simple example in the later stages was always, when taking Dad out the house, to have a back-up pack of spare disposal underpants, wet-wipes and plastic bags to cover any eventualities, while minimising their embarrassment: 'Nothing to worry about, Dad, all sorted, etc.'

As time progressed, Dad developed urinary tract infections (UTIs) which had a tendency to alter his mood and behaviour. This is well documented, yet Dad was not aware of their impact, and so the need became apparent to develop mitigations to keep Dad in a state of normality: 'It's all normal, Dad; here's some medication to help you with this.' Similarly, Dad struggled to use a knife and fork towards the end, and so to preserve his dignity we swapped to all of us using spoons when he was with us, or even resorted to finger food. Where funds permitted we happily let Dad rely on tea shops who were exemplary in their care and lookout for Dad, well versed in his condition and needs.

Allow the person, too, some grace in their decline as they become content with long periods of silence, quietly staring out of windows or falling asleep at no notice. Similarly, small, insignificant details became blown out of proportion and ended up being a fixation—it was necessary to develop distraction techniques on occasions in order to end transfixing spells and the hold they seemed to exert. Don't be angry with them: look past the disease.

Throughout it all were our best endeavours to help keep and maintain some independence within the grounds of safety and their ability to cope. We kept up a programme of events and day trips so as to maximise normality and enjoyment, and continued to focus on giving him some ability to feel like he was still in control, even in the bigger decisions: 'It needs to be one of these care homes, Dad; which one would you like it to be?'

To heighten the sense of normalcy we continued, too, to make the most of simple things—staying over at our house, enjoying a glass of wine in front of the fire, watching yet another a war film, with a blanket over his knees. These very simplest of pleasures were treasured by us and there was no doubt it was reciprocated.

Finally, rein in your expectation of what can be done. We were able in the early days to have a day trip on the Eurostar to Paris in late 2016 and somehow go down a coal mine in late 2018, but it was all while assessing his safety and ability to cope.

Chapter 6

Spiritual aspects

After my conversion while at university I settled into a local home church that held firmly to the solid, timeless biblical doctrines of God's sovereignty, His unique and total involvement in a person's salvation, all founded in and through the person of Jesus Christ. The Bible teaches there is only one God (1 Corinthians 8:6), to whom we owe everything: our lives, loves, hearts, souls and minds. We are the created, He is the Creator, and at the end of our one life He will rightly ask what we have done with it. His Son Jesus has been appointed as Judge, to settle once for all the consequences of sin in the world and our lives (Acts 17:31). We know we have fallen well short of His perfect standards and we need someone outside of ourselves to make amends, to make us clean, to pay our sin debt and to assuage His anger at our wrongdoing (Romans 3:25). Jesus is able to do all that for us: we simply need to turn to him for acceptance, forgiveness and cleansing. He is close by us, and offers each person, each uniquely made and precious person, that offer of salvation—full, free, unconditional, eternal.

As this began to be absorbed in my thinking in my early adult life, I began to see that the consequences of being outside of God's offer of salvation were disastrous. Outside of God in eternity is a darkness, a separation that cannot be crossed once we have passed over from this life (Luke 16:26). Realising the starkness of this binary choice I was galvanised into praying for loved ones around me, including my precious Dad. His view at the time was that it was some sort of 'phase' I was going through and that it would pass.

Spiritual aspects

Clearly months and years went by and Dad moved to a begrudging acceptance of my faith in God, all the while keeping up the message of 'I'm OK thanks, I'm a good person' mentality. From time to time I tried to puncture this world view, with somewhat clumsy attempts to witness to Dad. None of this seemed to have any impact on his outlook or lack of faith. I repeatedly sought to bring him to church, to evangelistic services at Christmas and Easter, where I would observe his general discomfort. There was still no change.

As the years went by, my growing sense of angst heightened, as I considered the thought, albeit briefly, in fleeting passing moments (I was too afraid to consider staring at it full on) that he was moving inexorably, yearly, towards some sort of end game. I remember clearly one day walking in London early one morning with a sense of anxiety as I knew, clearly, that a crunch time was coming. 'It's all a long way off,' was my way of dismissing the gnawing doubt.

Once he was diagnosed with dementia and once the pieces and awareness of the disease started to slot into place, I knew that the end game was suddenly in much sharper focus. This stepped up the angst in prayer, and really was the trigger to start to get me to pray both for his salvation and also for the practical levels of care needed. I began to wrestle more seriously with the significance of what Dad was going through, especially as I considered his mental capacity diminishing with regards to understanding and accepting God's offer of salvation. What then are the issues to consider and what tools does God gives us to face this crisis?

The call to care—how, why and what God expects

As we move to consider the needs of precious loved ones around us there is a certain innate sense that they need care, love and provision, and that in itself this does not need to be reasoned or verbalised; it feels 'right' or 'automatic' that we step up our involvement and care for those affected by this cruel disease.

Chapter 6

Nonetheless, it is helpful to frame the views of our heavenly Father on the topic of care and His particular charge on us close by. Some useful verses to consider include:

- Blessed are those who honour their mother and father (Exodus 20:12—a command tied up with a promise of long life, albeit framed in the Old Testament. We are not motivated to care and honour our parents *because* of the promise, as we do it as a matter of course, not for any reward or potential blessing). The promise is reiterated in Ephesians 6:2.

- God places the lonely in families (Psalm 68:6).

- Blessed are those who take care of widows (Deuteronomy 14:29; James 1:27).

- We are given gifts and strengths in order to serve God and people (such as the parable of the shrewd manager that Jesus told—Luke 16:1–13).

- God cares for people (consider Jesus' example of the good shepherd, where one lost sheep was sought out, over and above the ninety-nine that were all right—Matthew 18:12–14).

- We are to serve God (and our family or friend with dementia) with all our heart and soul, mind and strength (Matthew 22:37; Deuteronomy 6:4–7).

- Give us this day our daily bread (Matthew 6:11)—this shows us our total reliance on Him, and that we can depend on Him.

Spiritual aspects

As you transition into caring for your parents there is a sense that in some small way you are repaying the debt you owe them; as your parents cared for you, so you must now care for them. It is helpful to recognise that any funds and monies they have are for their care. You will care for them out of principle, not for any gain (Mark 7:9–13—honouring your parents).

This is a chance to reflect and mirror Jesus.

All these verses demonstrate our heavenly Father's loving care of ourselves and our loved ones around us. In fact, His care is far more powerful, forceful, resourceful, effective and strategic than anything done in our own strength; we are merely the instruments of His care, even when we feel weak and helpless in ourselves. As we step into the breach, He gives us grace to care.

On yourself

As you begin to grasp the size of the challenge and draw upon your personal resources, you will quickly realise the enormity of what is going on and the total inadequacy of your wisdom, strength, courage and love needed to help the person you are caring for. The sooner the dawn of this realisation, the quicker you will come to an end of yourself and cry out before your heavenly Father that you cannot do this task (Exodus 18:18—Moses was made to realise that the task was too much for him). Be prepared for God to work, for Him to show his mighty strength (Psalm 68:28) and for Him to work (act) for those who wait for Him (Isaiah 64:4).

You will need superhuman levels of resource, wisdom and grace—so come to your heavenly Father, whose storehouses are full (Malachi 3:10) and who is both able and willing to help in this commission (1 Thessalonians 5:24).

You will have your faith tested, stretched and magnified. God will do wonderful things to those who trust Him and commit their ways to Him (Proverbs 3:5–6). You will see first-hand His

Chapter 6

provision; your own personal faith will be increased (John 11:40). You will also be blessed in other ways (Psalm 119:67,71). Friends will be drawn into your circle of care and you will be uniquely bound to them for the shared experience you will go through. Your family, too, will watch and witness God at work—to Him be the glory (*soli deo gratia*).

Utterly rely on Him—Matthew 6:34—trust Him for each day, one day at a time. He knows the daily bread you need—seek Him for this.

On your family (if you have one)

While wrestling the additional care needs of another, there still remains the need and duty of care for surrounding family. This responsibility does not go away, even though at many times I got the balance wrong.

Talk to them about what is going on. Explain the additional pull on your time. Involve them in praying for the person with dementia and outline to them the spiritual struggles that are going on. They will surprise you with their maturity, compassion, insight and prayerfulness.

At the same time there may need to be a conscious handing over of the family to the Lord. He knows the way that you (and they) take (Job 13:15). He is able to keep them, as the author of their faith (Hebrews 12:2), and is able to make all grace abound to them (2 Corinthians 9:8).

You still need to shepherd them while leading them through this process—this is a test of their faith as much as it is of yours.

The Bible's view of dementia

Turning, then, to what God reveals to us in the Scriptures, what does He say about the decline and passing of a person affected by dementia? Obviously, such a condition was not described in the

Spiritual aspects

Bible, although some episodes appear where people diminished in their physical capabilities (Eli was 90 years old and blind when he died). Nonetheless, the principles of God's view can be used to help us understand at some level what is going on and what, importantly, is God's view of someone affected with dementia.

Death, decay and decline are not a part of the world order (John 11:35; Isaiah 25:7–8)—it feels an unnatural process because it *is* an un-natural process. It riles us, disturbs us, affronts us, makes us angry. Coupled with it is the loss of dignity that goes with it. Notice, though, how much Jesus went out of his way to show love and dignity to these needing his critical help around him.

Jesus wept at the graveside of Lazarus. Consider his compassion on the widow's son, Peter's mother-in-law, etc. Death is not the natural world order—it is an affront, an enemy. Be angry—it's right. Look at Joseph's grief at the passing of his father Jacob (Genesis 50:1).

The person

Gnawing away at the evangelical heart is the awareness of what God's Word says about being lost. It is unequivocal. Sobering passages highlight that we live once only (Hebrews 9:27) and after death must give account of our life to God's appointed Judge (Acts 17:31). Sin is a real, terrible affront to our holy God and cannot go unpunished (Romans 6:23). Those who die in their sin, unconfessed, unforgiven, face an eternity outside of God's blessing and presence (2 Thessalonians 1:9). Jesus calls this place hell, from which there is no subsequent escape (Luke 16:19–31). To pass therefore from this life without your sin dealt with is, ultimately, to be lost. It is desperate. Forever so.

Praise God, however, for his compassion on the lost alive today—Jesus came to offer a permanent rescue from this disaster! Thank you, Lord!

Chapter 6

Having this knowledge does two things. Firstly, it makes us desperate for the person concerned to turn to Jesus and accept his forgiveness. We will want to share this with the person with dementia as much and as carefully and as timely as we can. And, secondly, we will pray. If only you could flick a switch in someone's heart and they would believe! But it doesn't work like that. God designed it so. He clearly says, some plant the seed, others water it, but only God can make it grow (1 Corinthians 3:6–7). Pray, above all, pray. Have seasons of special prayer and fasting if you are able. I recall on one occasion shouting at God, as I was desperate for an intervention in my Dad's care and for God's wisdom. My prayers rotated around Dad's care, his medication, his practical needs and support and his salvation. Covet the prayers of others. Above all, come to your heavenly Father, who knows where you are and what you are going through (Job 13:15).

Next, consider the advice of others. How have they dealt and coped in their spiritual crisis of witnessing to others? Seek out help, including from your pastor, on how to share the gospel. I went to see our pastor on an unrelated matter and he ended up sharing about the thief on the cross, as there, in that narrative, is the gospel boiled down to the absolute essentials only (more of that later).

I recall reading accounts of former pastors and ministers who over long years had witnessed to many hundreds of people who, near their end of life or even in their final hours seemingly, had not shown much sign of responding. As people lived unconverted, so they died unconverted, entrenched in their sin and unbelief. There is only one account in the whole of Scripture of a person being saved at end of life. So we must not presume on God being patient and allowing a plentiful last minute salvation.

Others, well documented historically, had encountered many cases where people had appeared to be at end of life and had indeed seemed to have responded to God's call to claim the name

Spiritual aspects

of Jesus for their forgiveness and salvation; these people had then recovered back to a measure of health, but the clear majority had returned to their former ways of seemingly unconverted living—their confessions had merely been superficial at the time, with no depth or sincerity.

The knowledge of these situations further compounded the desperateness of the situation with my Dad, starring at an upcoming, imminent disaster. Yet one example there was in the Bible to hold on to: the thief on the cross. So we might hold on to hope, even in the valley of the shadow of death.

Scriptures to help you—encouraging you on the way

- Hebrews 11:6. 'And without faith it is impossible to please God, because anyone who comes to Him must believe that *He exists* and that *He rewards those who earnestly seek Him*' (my emphasis).

- Habakkuk 3:17–19. 'Though the fig tree does not bud and there are no grapes on the vines, though the olive crop fails and the fields produce no food, though there are no sheep in the pen and no cattle in the stalls, yet I will rejoice in the LORD; I will be joyful in God my Saviour. The Sovereign LORD is my strength; He makes my feet like the feet of a deer, He enables me to tread on the heights.'

- Luke 18:4–8 (The Persistent Widow). '"Even though I don't fear God or care about men, yet because this widow keeps bothering me, I will see that she gets justice, so that she won't eventually wear me out with her coming!" And the Lord said, "Listen to what the unjust judge says. And will not God bring about justice for His chosen ones, who cry out to Him day and night? Will He keep putting them off? I tell you, He will see that they get justice, and quickly."'

Chapter 6

- Psalm 126 (the whole psalm).

- Psalm 119:105. 'Your word is a lamp to my feet and a light for my path.'

- Malachi 3:6. 'I the LORD do not change. So you, O descendants of Jacob, are not destroyed.'

- Job 13:15. 'Though he slay me, yet will I hope in him; I will surely defend my ways to his face.'

- Job 23:10. 'But He knows the way that I take; when He has tested me, I shall come forth as gold.'

Scriptures and words to use in witness

Realising the crisis that was looming on the horizon, I arranged a meeting with a wise and trusted Christian friend, Neil, one lunchtime at Euston Station. There I confronted him with my worst fears—what if God doesn't save my Dad? How can I go on in my faith? How can I tell others of the love of Christ, knowing it wasn't seemingly strong enough to save my Dad? How can I encourage others to pray if God didn't hear my own prayer? I wasn't threatening to walk away from my faith, but I could see the make-or-break impact this could cause. My friend wisely didn't directly answer this question but instead helped equip me with the tools to witness to my Dad, to harness me to greater action with whatever opportunities still lay open.

Neil's advice, over some sort of falafel burger (yuck …!), was for me to sit down with Dad with no distractions, look him in the eye with my hand on his face, and engage him with heartfelt earnestness saying, 'Dad, you need to know how much we love you. As you enter the final chapter of your life, I need to speak to you. This life

Spiritual aspects

isn't everything, and once it is over we pass into God's presence. I know I will be with Him for ever and I want you to be with me forever. It's really simple; you can be with me and Jesus for ever. Ask Him to be your Lord.'

Neil continued: 'God has spared your Dad thus far and given you these feelings for a reason.' Pride was the biggest obstacle to my Dad having faith and Neil encouraged me to shameless audacity in prayer (like the widow in Luke 18), giving God no rest, even though God had not forgotten my Dad or me. I needed the Holy Spirit to laser through the fog of confusion in my Dad's mind. Dementia is no barrier to the Holy Spirit working in a person; the gospel is not limited.

At around the same time I went to see my pastor on an unrelated matter and we got round to speaking about the thief on the cross (Luke 23:39–43). The gospel is right there, distilled down to the very basics, but it is enough. The three steps of the thief's response were:

(i) I've not lived a perfect life.
(ii) Jesus, you're a King who's done nothing wrong.
(iii) Will you have me in your kingdom?

Those simple statements and question were sufficient to show a changed heart, a simple understanding had been realised and a public request of faith—it was utterly sufficient. Jesus replied: 'Truly I tell you, today you will be with Me in paradise' (Luke 23:43).

Armed with these conversations I went to see my Dad and delivered my message. There was no real response other than a mumbled, 'I'll consider it,' reply and certainly no immediate change. But it did help me, albeit by a small amount, to realise I had done what I could. It really was down to the Lord to save him now.

Other spiritual helps

I found out that a beloved, devoted, Christian couple from a local church had befriended Dad and had started visiting him during the

Chapter 6

week, unrequested by myself. Dad had been dragged to their annual Christmas service (largely by me) and over the years had gotten to know this couple; now they were visiting him and taking the initiative, popping round frequently to see how he was. They shared a few verses with him and prayed with him. He told me about '… those people … they were here again … we did a whatisit …', to which I would smile, knowing they were reading God's Word to him. Blessed are the feet of those who bring good news (Isaiah 52:7). 'Use your best weapons' was the response I got from a friend when I told him about this couple's visit. Some plant the seed, others water, but only God makes it grow (1 Corinthians 3:6–7).

As mentioned previously, prepare what to say. Be prepared to say it more than once, but not in an overbearing manner, nor forcing it upon them. Pray for the opportunity to say something, to share something of God's Word or a few thoughts of testimony. Do it sooner rather than later. Memorise passages. We brought my Dad a large print Bible, so he had access to one. My daughter, when visiting, would highlight verses and leave it open for Dad to read.

How to pray

Without doubt your sense of helplessness is there to drive you to pray. When all is said and done, and strength and wisdom are exhausted, then we must turn to the one true source of hope, strength and wisdom: our heavenly Father. He can work. And in this crucible you may have first-hand experience to see that.

So, what to pray?

Lord, grant me courage. Grant a sense of expectation and equipping for each day, as I face the unknown, making it up as I go along. Stand in the gap, with arms raised, like Moses. There's a famous quote, attributed to William Carey: 'Speak to God for man, and speak to man for God.' Ask that the Lord would move towards

Spiritual aspects

mercy. Remind Him that He takes no pleasure in the death of a sinner. Pray with others, including your family. 'Jesus, you are the Good Shepherd, please go and seek out this lost sheep.'

Some verses to help guide your prayers:

- Lamentations 3:26. 'It is good to wait quietly for the salvation of the LORD.'

- Ezekiel 36:26. 'I will give you a new heart and put a new spirit in you; I will remove from you your heart of stone and give you a heart of flesh.'

- 1 Corinthians 3:6-8. You plant the seed, others water it, but only God can make it grow.

A devout Christian lady made a bold, somewhat revelatory statement to me as the crisis deepened, as she'd concluded after caring for her own mum: 'God used dementia to save my mum.' It took me by surprise on many levels, but I came to hang on to that statement on many occasions.

Pray too for yourself: 'Lord, what do I need to learn through this?' He won't necessarily remove you out of the situation but will give sufficient grace (2 Corinthians 12:9). God doesn't make mistakes—this is a circumstance and a place for a season that you will pass through. In the end, the entire episode is for God; He is the centre of all that is happening with your suffering friend or relative. God stores your tears in his bottle (Psalm 56:8).

Further witnessing

What evidence are you looking for? Surely some sort of turning towards God, some acknowledgement of faith. It may not be a

Chapter 6

full confession of faith, but you are looking for some sort of acknowledgement. When my own pastor came to visit my Dad in his last few days as I witnessed and prayed with Dad, by way of response Dad, not able to speak, nonetheless held his hands together in a form of prayer, at which my pastor said, 'Are you calling out to Jesus?' and there was a definite positive movement of acknowledgement.

Other verses were used and read to Dad, including John 3:16, Isaiah 43:1–5, Psalm 145:17–20.

The thief on the cross was able to articulate the simplest response of faith. A simple, heartfelt 'Amen' is sufficient. A friend of mine, Peter, gave an account concerning his own father who passed away several years before in similar circumstances. His father wasn't a believer, and Peter had prayed and witnessed to him many times. But even in the last few days he still wasn't sure if his Dad had turned to the Lord. Early that morning, as his Dad was passing, Peter, in the room with him, kept saying 'Go to Jesus, Dad.' Even after he had died, believing that the spirit remains for a short while, Peter had continued with the statement, 'Go to Jesus, Dad.' Utterly broken, Peter drove home and prayed, 'Lord, if my Dad didn't make it I don't want to know right now.' Arriving home, Peter's son opened the door, and before Peter had a chance to say anything his son stated he'd just had a vivid dream where he'd seen Jesus and his Grandad (Peter's Dad) walking together along a beach. He'd had the dream about the time that Peter's Dad had passed away.

My pastor shared a story about his own uncle who was in a coma for the last six weeks of his life. On visiting one day he'd said to his uncle, 'I'm going to pray now.' 'OK' was the response from his seemingly unconscious uncle, followed by a remarkable 'Amen' at the end of the prayer. This was the last time they heard him speak.

I counter all this with the well-established school of thought that not many are saved in old age or at life's end. There should be no

Spiritual aspects

presumption of salvation. Some ministers have reflected on their own death-bed witnessing, that few genuinely appear to be saved. Those that did, upon making some sort of recovery went back to their former life of unbelief. As mentioned, the Bible has only one example of a person saved at the end of their life (the thief on the cross).

I witnessed, prayed, and wrestled for my own mother's salvation but had no evidence in the end that she was saved. Nor my aunt. A friend recounted many years ago that his own grandad, on his death bed, pointedly and terrifyingly stated he wanted nothing to do with 'that God stuff'. God isn't going to save everyone.

Perhaps your prayer could be, 'Lord, give me something to hold on to.' Jesus will not drive away those who come to Him.

Chapter 7

End days

After nearly six months of full-time live-in care support Dad became much weaker and struggled to get up and down the stairs in his house. Liaising with the carer it was clear we were moving towards some sort of end game. Dad increasingly woke in the night. He began to struggle with simple things like eating using any sort of cutlery. His movements became very slow. He drifted in and out of sleeping more often and conversations were very muted. Nights were much more subject to broken sleep for Dad and therefore for the carer. In early July we managed to get him down to his beloved Dorset for a weekend, in what sadly proved to be the last time. We knew it, too.

In mid-August he stayed for one last night at our house. We had takeaway fish and chips and ate with our fingers so as to not make him feel awkward. The carer was taking Dad to more and more day centres. In the background I started making more plans for a care home, feeling that this time Dad had little strength to resist. We considered two teams of live-in carers, one for the day, one for the night, and we considered moving him to live downstairs in his house, which would have entailed significant structural changes. Needing such intensive care made the decision simpler to have him move to a care home, with all the bespoke, specialist care it provided. I looked around for a new, more suitable care home, and found one a few miles from our home and quietly made the arrangements, signing a contract, making preparations for Dad to move in. We organised for the carer to take Dad there for a visit

End days

for several hours, so that, Dad unsuspecting, they could assess him. They were happy to take him.

Before that could happen, however, Dad took a serious turn for the worse and ended up being admitted to A & E. We dashed back from a weekend away, and upon arriving at hospital I was taken aside by one of the triage doctors and told Dad might not pull through and that they would not be attempting to resuscitate him. This was a considerable shock to be confronted with. After several days of touch and go he pulled through and slowly started responding to antibiotics and the medical care and attention received. We made considerable effort to get him out of bed, as everybody had said this was vital to any sort of recovery; once they don't get out of bed, that's it. After some desperate attempts we got him to stand under his own weight and rewarded him with a quick wheelchair trip outside of the building, to help him rekindle some life.

People were praying for Dad and us. Some dear Christian friends came to visit him in hospital. I arranged, optimistically, for him to be transferred from hospital to the care home. To our surprise he rallied enough, and both the hospital and care home agreed to the transfer. All the preparations were made to make his room seem homely, with pictures, clothing and music to seem like his own place. The live-in carer was retained for a week to help with the transition.

On the day of the transfer, the hospital transferred Dad, accompanied by the carer, to the home. We arrived later to help him settle, and the care home happily allowed me to sleep the night on a put-up bed in Dad's room with him. A broken night's sleep followed, but it did at least give Dad some assurance and peace of mind. He could tell he wasn't in his own home.

I briefed the care home on Dad's habits, tastes, preferences and stocked them up with medicines and things he would need. I arranged a cash float for them. We made the room as homely and

Chapter 7

familiar as possible. We told his neighbours and the local deli (that he'd virtually lived in for years) where he was and encouraged them to visit. We agreed care visit hours with them and the wider family. I tried to visit daily in the week, after work, so as to check up on the level of care and attention he was receiving and also to reassure Dad that this was the new normal.

His world now was very small. He didn't leave the care home premises. He would sit out in the garden for periods of time during the day and I would help get him ready for bed in the evening. The carer visited daily ('Where've you been?' said an exasperated Dad, unaware how dependent he now was), and then at the end of his week the carer said he was going away for a bit (which was true, as he took a well-earned overseas trip for a break).

Deep down, Dad knew he was in care. He knew too that he was declining. Conversation was entirely one-way. Physio was arranged, privately, so as to help Dad recover some strength. Distant family came down for a brief weekend visit. He managed to eat tiny amounts of liquefied meals and we desperately struggled to get him to take fluids. He lost weight and looked very gaunt, pale and tired.

After two weeks in care he was making tiny incremental improvements in eating, sitting up and physio. Several times when I'd visited him I noticed him welling up and then hiding his face. 'I don't believe it,' he said, recognising me on one visit. I recall the last time he said my name. I visited him on a Thursday evening just as his evening physio was starting, so I helped with him moving up out of his chair and out into the garden. He seemed brighter, although he couldn't swallow a cup of tea; I told myself that he'd be all right and in good hands while I had a cycling weekend away in Devon, a brief respite from the strain. After I left him that evening I subsequently found out that Dad had summoned a superhuman amount of strength and by himself, at his own initiative, had got

End days

himself up and managed to walk unaided and unprompted out to the garden and back, to the surprise of the care staff.

Events, however, turned out much worse as by the Saturday afternoon family were making desperate attempts to reach me in Devon to get me to return urgently as Dad had deteriorated and was now bed-bound, too weak to move. With limited trains available I had no choice but to return first thing Sunday morning, via taxi, train and a friend's kind lift from Reading station. From then on in it was a bedside vigil, rotated among the family by Dad's side.

I slept the Sunday night in his room, speaking to him in his brief moments of being awake. Our pastor visited and witnessed and prayed with Dad. Dad's hands were clasped together in a prayer response to the pastor's invitation to turn and accept Jesus.

We all prayed with and shared passages of Scripture with Dad. We pulled the children out of school on the Monday for a visit, as much for them as for Dad. He was awake briefly for their visit, smiling when I mentioned my daughter's name, and turning his head towards my son as he read to him. We arranged a friend who serves in a Christian care home as a pastoral chaplain, to visit Dad and give end of life witness. We were aware that many, many folks were praying. Dad slipped in and out of consciousness, sleeping much of the time. He lost the ability to speak. His eyes were open all the time, but clearly his sight went. We'd been encouraged to keep on talking, holding his hand, as hearing is the last sense to be lost (in some measure perhaps of divine last grace). We told him we loved him and thanked him for being Dad. All was forgiven from our side.

In the last week or so I'd been alone with Dad and had yet another go at challenging him. I witnessed to him and then we both said a prayer together. I prayed the thief on the cross prayer: 'Lord we've not been perfect. Lord Jesus, you are a King, who's done nothing wrong…'. At this point I was interrupted by Dad, who had never said anything in my praying—he cut across my words, saying,

Chapter 7

'That's true …'. I was dumbfounded … and elated at his simple faith statement. It was another small evidence that God was working in Dad's heart.

The bedside rotating vigil continued—I recall driving back to the care home at 3 am, tears choked back as I knew this was the last time. As I drove, praying, I recalled Jesus' tears at the grave-side of his friend Lazarus, and knew Jesus was with us in the final precious hours. He belonged to God and it was God's prerogative to order the timing. My final refrain to him, over and over, was 'Turn to Jesus, Dad. Walk to Jesus.' Surrounded by his son, daughter, partner and daughter-in-law, Dad passed from this life early on the Wednesday morning, I believe into God's presence, as an accepted child of God. Like the thief on the cross, he had taken the bare minimum of faith steps. All his resistance and barriers evaporated and gone, in simple child-like faith, he had crossed over during his final weeks and days. To God be the glory.

Chapter 8

Afterwards

The silence of Dad's passing was akin to the centre of a storm, the very eye of the hurricane. In complete bewilderment and daze we quietly said goodbye and left him in the care of the home to make plans with the funeral directors and doctor. My wife and I returned home to break the tragic news to our suspecting children. Immediately afterwards we went out for a breakfast at a local garden centre, by way of something mindless to do. It was a time of total numbness and loss at the gaping void left by his departure. Later that day we went to his house—for what? I'm not even sure.

Appointments were made with the local registrar, doctor's notes were obtained, and further calls and arrangements made. We agreed a meeting with a local funeral director and fielded calls. Suddenly there was growing list of things to think about, which totally took over. Many decisions were called for—burial or cremation, where and how to have a funeral service—which in turn were a minefield of people's choices and requirements. And yet also they were perhaps a welcome distraction. Dad's will had been chased repeatedly and was only finally sent to us by email on the day he passed away.

The sense of duty and expectation returned as decisions were needed. Conscious again that many were upholding us in prayer and that in fact the Lord was carrying us through, a friend texted that Jesus was enough—our sure and only anchor.

Many difficult challenges remained: clearing his clothing and possessions from the care home, finding addresses of people to

Chapter 8

contact, choosing hymns, caterers, flowers, and so on. Take time to cope with yourself, as the numbness continues for many weeks.

I told my employer of the news and they kindly sent cards, flowers and well wishes. As I'd used up most of compassionate leave I was forced to return to work. In hindsight I should have gone straight to my GP for a two-week sick note.

Rely on your family and friends; take up their offers of help, even for the small mundane things. Rely too on the Lord, even when you feel you can't pray. Words, groans and sighs are enough.

Seasons of great sadness will follow. Often at strange moments, such as when building IKEA furniture, with a sudden, compelling forcefulness, it hit me that Dad had 'gone'. Or on the train to work I would realise that no more would I go to certain places that I used to with Dad. The door has closed to that. They were happy days that were now irrecoverably removed. Be prepared for the strength of that loss to hit you.

As the funeral came and went I started to realise that the focus had been on me (and my suffering and sadness) and my loss. The eulogy took considerable effort to craft, write and balance it. I had to break free from some of this and plead with the Lord. My realisation and prayer was for Him to show me and change me from making other people, even a close, precious Dad, an idol, even dear relatives, people we have looked up to and relied upon as pillars and rocks, people in the very centre of our hearts, people we have lived our lives for. Forgive us Lord, as You should be there.

The night before Dad passed away, I was on the phone to a dear brother as he was heading into his home group, and I relayed to him what was happening and the work I believe God had done. My friend Peter remarked how astounding that was, and that God had honoured the prayers of many. Consequently, his challenge to me was the need to follow up with witnessing to others, to take the boldness to go and witness.

Afterwards

Practical matters will drain you of time, energy and focus, like the challenge of making funeral payments and following the legal process. Keep your reserves of strength and pace yourself, so as to be what you need to be. You will not accomplish everything quickly; rather, take a slow, steady, systematic approach. A friend, when his own mother died, wrote a long list of things to do, and as he crossed them off more actions came to mind and were added to the bottom of the list. Many, many things will need to be done, people contacted, issues closed out, items disposed of, ashes buried, memorials arranged.

In the meantime, don't alienate your family but rather involve them in the process as far as they are able. People will understand your unavailability. Lots of well-meaning people will show many surprising acts of kindness, even to the simple offer of meeting at the pub one evening to talk about whatever. Take them up on these offers. God will uphold you.

Take a holiday, if means permit, to help pause and reflect on what has happened, and to get some horizon and perspective. Seek professional help for yourself, especially if you immerse yourself in the daily grind and know that you are not dealing with the underlying grief. Encourage those around you to do likewise. Don't focus on the last days; give thanks for who the person was.

Do a half marathon or have some such physical, external, goal to focus on: something to help you give back and to look outwards.

In the rawness of the aftermath, and later, as things calmed a bit, I frequently asked if I could have done more. It was a difficult question to answer and one that could not easily be sidestepped. Those things are now done, closed out and cannot much be changed. Rather, get together with others to hear more about your loved one, and learn new stories and anecdotes about them.

Aware that I had some tentative evidence that Dad had been saved in his last days, turning to the Lord, I started documenting the basis

Chapter 8

for that hope. I recalled all the conversations, text messages and encouragements that people had shared with me, both before and after Dad's passing. The list of evidence was much longer than I had anticipated, giving a measure of comfort that Dad was safe with Jesus. It included my pastor, two former pastors, the beloved couple who regularly witnessed to him, my wife's assertion, the measure of peace Dad had in passing, the scriptures and prayers shared that elicited a positive acknowledgement from him. Individually they could be dismissed, discounted maybe as positive, hopeful thinking; collectively they formed a more compelling picture that Dad had indeed accepted and called out to Jesus in his last days. He said some clear 'amens' in the last days.

Perhaps God saves people at the last, but does not let them recover and return to their old ways; rather He takes them at the face value of a simple faith statement and that is good enough for Him. I do believe so. All who come to Him (Jesus), He will not cast out.

Sadly, they were always going to pass away; while there is the huge loss of dignity and faculty, maybe God was using that to give the person one last chance to turn to Him, to accept Jesus in a simple way. As I noted in my eulogy—God removed the barriers of doubt and resistance in Dad's heart, and in a very simple way, Dad was enabled to say 'Amen' to the sinner's prayer. Looking back, God was masterfully preparing all the circumstances to lead to that moment, preparing both Dad and us and those around us for that moment. Tracing the evidence of that backwards, we could see the line of circumstances stretching many months and in fact years back, all leading to Dad's outcome of embryonic faith … moving everything into place, moving people to cry to Him, on His throne, to act and save.

The Lord doesn't remove the loss, the pain of separation. He has His ways and remains in many aspects inscrutable. And yet He is full of compassion (Isaiah 30:18).

Afterwards

As mentioned previously, I felt prompted to start to draft this advice in the apparent vacuum of other suitable literature to help. I started this book before Dad passed away and completed it afterwards.

Recently an image came to mind that Dad was heading over a large waterfall, in a small helpless boat, carried over by the unstoppable current. We could see it happening. Yet Jesus was there with him in the boat.

Every case of dementia is different. This is neither a template nor blueprint for how to cope. But hopefully some of it will encourage you, equip you and point to what God is doing.

Trust God with your grief—Jesus is enough.

Acknowledgements and reference material

Throughout this process I wish to acknowledge with grateful thanks my own church who supported me, the family and my Dad in prayer and with cards, visits, messages and encouragements. Thank you for your deep, loving, faithful, genuine concern. You know who you are.

Thank you, too, for the care home, care agencies, carers, support services, neighbours, doctors, and other medical professionals who all stepped in at various times to assist. You know who you are.

Thank you, too, to the Christian friends who had stood by, prayed, visited and witnessed to Dad. Some plant the seed and others water it—thank you. You, too, know who you are.

Thank you too, for my loving family, in accepting my long absences in caring for Dad, witnessing first-hand the strain on myself and the difficulty they too experienced.

Finally, all thanks ultimately must centre back to God, for His intervention, planning, purpose, compassion and love, to strengthen us, impart wisdom, and for His saving work. To Him be the glory.

Acknowledgements and reference material

Helpful books

Hallesby, O., *Prayer*
Lewis, C. S., *A Grief Observed*
Dunn, Ronald, *When Heaven is Silent*
When Someone Dies: A Practical Guide by Care
    ISBN: 978-0-905195-13-1
Morse, Louise, *What Matters In The End*
    ISBN 978-0-9930148-9-5

Reference websites and materials to use

www.alzheimers.org.uk
www.desiringgod.org
www.cqc.org.uk
www.carersuk.org
www.ageuk.org.uk